Jordan
in pictures

A farmer loads his tank truck with precious water from a catchment area. The mule looks as though he would like a drink.

by CAMILLE MIREPOIX STEGMULLER

**VISUAL
GEOGRAPHY
SERIES**

STERLING PUBLISHING CO., INC. NEW YORK
Oak Tree Press Co., Ltd.
London & Sydney

VISUAL GEOGRAPHY SERIES

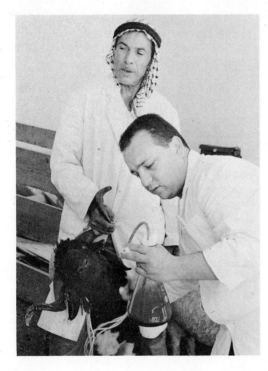

A Bedouin brings one of his sheep to an animal health clinic for a blood test. The Bedouin at least seems cheerful about it.

Copyright © 1974 by Sterling Publishing Co., Inc.
419 Park Avenue South, New York, N.Y. 10016
British edition published by Oak Tree Press Co., Ltd., Nassau, Bahamas
Distributed in Australia and New Zealand by Oak Tree Press Co., Ltd.,
P.O. Box J34, Brickfield Hill, Sydney 2000, N.S.W.
Distributed in the United Kingdom and elsewhere in the British Commonwealth
by Ward Lock Ltd., 116 Baker Street, London W 1
Manufactured in the United States of America   *All rights reserved*
Library of Congress Catalog Card No.: 74–82330
Sterling ISBN 0–8069–1186–7 Trade   Oak Tree 7061–2035–3
1187–5 Library

CONTENTS

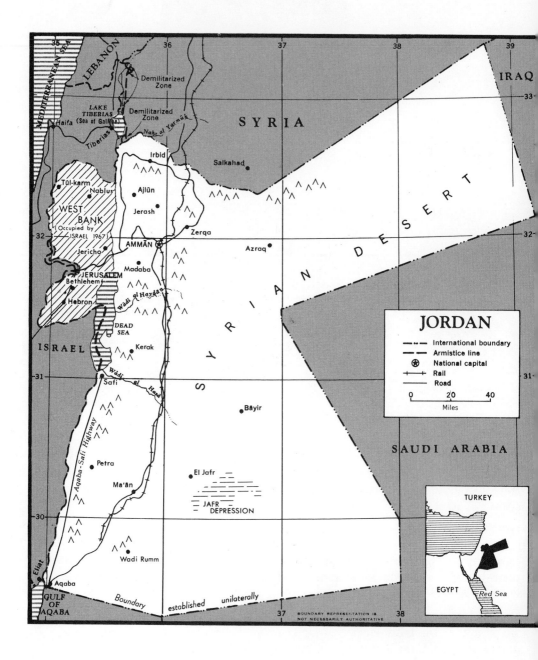

PICTURE CREDITS

The publishers wish to thank the following for the use of the photographs in this book: John Fistere and Associates, Beirut, Lebanon; Albert Flouty, Amman, Jordan; Jordan Ministry of Information, Amman; Jordan Ministry of Tourism and Antiquities, Amman; Jordan Tourism Authority, Amman; Jordan Tourist Information Center, Beirut; Photo Manoug, Beirut; Camille Mirepoix Stegmuller; Hagop Toranian, Amman; United Nations, New York; United Nations Relief and Works Agency for Palestine Refugees.

In Jordan's Baq'a Valley, near Amman, an extensive agricultural project has been started. These camels employed by the project are heading for a waterhole after the day's work.

I. THE LAND

THE HASHEMITE KINGDOM of Jordan is bounded on the north by Syria, on the east by Iraq, on the southeast and south by Saudi Arabia, and on the west by Israel and by the Israeli-occupied West Bank region, part of Jordan until 1967. Jordan proper, which lies east of the Jordan River, has an area of 35,000 square miles (88,000 sq. km.), while the West Bank area has about 2,640 square miles (6,600 sq. km.). The total area of Jordan is about the same as that of Indiana, or of Scotland and Wales combined. Jordan's short 12 miles (19 km.) of coastline lies in the southwest on the Gulf of Aqaba, an arm of the Red Sea. The city of Aqaba, the only port, plays a large part in the economic life of the country.

SURFACE FEATURES

Jordan has four major geographical regions— the East Bank Uplands, the West Bank Uplands, the Jordan Desert and the Jordan Rift Valley. The Desert, located in the territory of the East Bank, taking up about four fifths of its space, is part of the Syrian Desert. Its northern part is composed of volcanic lava and basalt, and its southern part of sandstone and granite, partly eroded by wind. The East Bank Uplands overlook the Rift Valley and have an altitude of between 2,000 and 3,000 feet (600 and 900 metres) increasing in elevation to about 5,750 feet (1,725 metres) in the south. Outcrops of chalk, sand, limestone and flint extend to the

Young visitors on the shore of the Dead Sea read about where they are in English and Arabic.

extreme south, where igneous rocks predominate. Many valleys and streams circulate east, west and north while south of Al-karak, seasonal streams run east into a low region known as the Jafr Depression.

The Jordan Valley, almost 1,300 feet (390 metres) below sea level at the Dead Sea, is the lowest point on the surface of the earth. As it travels south, the Jordan River drains the waters of the Sea of Galilee, the Yarmuk River and the valley streams of both plateaus, into the Dead Sea. Actually a lake, the Dead Sea is 45 miles (72 km.) long by 10 miles (16 km.) wide — its waters are far saltier than the ocean.

The West Bank Uplands, known for centuries as the Samarian and Judean Mountains, have an average height of 3,000 feet (900 metres) above sea level. Several large valleys cut into them and drain west towards the Mediterranean; the valleys draining east are shorter, many consisting of deep gorges with soils both thin and poor, though occasional rich alluvial deposits are found among the hills.

In the Dead Sea area, a farmer carries home brush which he has gathered— with the help of his donkey and camel.

A Bedouin and his grandson stand on the summit of Mount Nebo. Their light, loose clothing protects them from the brilliant desert sun and allows cool air to circulate close to their bodies.

CLIMATE

The climate of Jordan is generally arid, varying from a pleasant Mediterranean type in the western part to desert heat in the east. Jericho, on the West Bank, 492 feet (150 metres) below sea level, ranges in temperature between 61° and 90° F. (15.6° and 32° C.) while in Amman, the monthly temperatures range from 44° to 87° F. (7° to 30° C.). The prevailing winds throughout the land are westerly to southwesterly. The short cool winters (very pleasant) have an average rainfall from 16 inches (40 cm.) in the north to 4 inches (10 cm.) in the south, while the Jordan Valley has about 8 inches (20 cm.) a year. In the Uplands, frost and snow occur in small amounts, but this seldom happens in the Rift Valley.

NATURAL RESOURCES

Jordan is fortunate in having a number of mineral resources, including huge deposits of limestone and phosphates, as well as iron, phosphorus, manganese and copper. Recently discovered minerals of importance include barite, quartzite, gypsum (used as fertilizer) and feldspar. Countless brightly hued marbles are quarried and used for decoration on pottery and on new buildings.

THE JORDAN RIVER

The Jordan River is revered by Christians, Jews and Moslems alike, and it is in its waters that Christ was baptized by St. John the Baptist. The Jordan has often been an international boundary and since 1948 has marked part of the frontier between Israel to the west and Jordan to the east, from a few miles south of the Sea of Galilee to the point where the Yabis

Modern electronic equipment is being used in the search for mineral resources.

In the Baq'a Valley, abundant water for irrigation is now being extracted from wells. The water runs off the surrounding mountains into the sandy soil to a depth of almost 250 feet (75 metres), where it is held by a vast bowl-shaped formation of hard rock.

composed of papyrus, water lilies and other pond flowers once filled the area, which was drained in the 1950's to form agricultural land.

Projects have been planned that embrace the waters of the entire basin. A proposal is being considered to maintain the level of the Dead Sea by channelling in salt water from the Mediterranean—at the same time using the flow to generate hydro-electricity. Because of the Arab-Israeli tensions, only a partial use of Jordan's waters have been made. Syria and Jordan look to the future construction of an irrigation and hydro-electric dam on the Yarmuk River, which forms a small part of their border before entering the Jordan.

River flows into it. Since 1967, however, when Israeli forces occupied Jordanian territory on the West Bank, the Jordan River has served as the cease-fire line as far as the Dead Sea. While 223 miles (357 km.) in length, its course meanders, and the beeline distance between its origin and the Dead Sea is roughly 124 miles (200 km.).

At one time the Greeks called the river the Aulon, the Hebrews knew it as al-Yardon but to the Arabs it is still thought of as ash-Shariah, meaning the Watering Place. The river has three principal sources, all of which rise at the foot of Mount Hermon. The longest one is the Hasbani, rising in Lebanon at a height of 1,800 feet (540 metres). From the east in Syria, flows the Nahr Baniyas, and between the two is the Dan, with its sparkling fresh water. These three rivers join together in the Hula Basin, into which other streams flow, the most noted being the Enot Enan. Dense vegetation

Concrete conduits cut down on the evaporation of the water they carry and help to make the desert bloom.

The ancient art of falconry, hunting with trained hawks, is still practiced in Jordan.

FLORA AND FAUNA

Flowering plants found in Jordan include poppies, roses, anemones, tamarisks and buckthorn.

There are about 35,000 acres (14,000 hectares) of forest in Jordan, most of it growing on the rocky highlands of the East Bank. In spite of heavy wood-cutting by villagers and heavy grazing by Bedouin flocks of sheep, the forest trees have not been thinned out as much as might be expected, due to the reforestation scheme commenced in 1948 by the Jordanian government. Predominant types of trees are the Aleppo and Kermes oak, the Palestine pistachio, and the Aleppo pine tree. Olives grow wild in many places, and the Phoenicia Juniper grows in the areas of lesser rainfall. The grasslands offer lean fare to the livestock, while on the East Bank they have been depleted to make way for land now devoted to olive and fruit trees. To increase the fertility of the pastures, artesian wells have been dug.

The wildlife of Jordan includes animals of

Goats graze on the slopes of Mount Nebo, where Moses once stood and looked upon the Promised Land.

9

The city of Amman spreads out over seven hills.

Ancient Amman has grown modern rapidly in recent years—many new residential quarters like this have been built.

both African and Asian types—jackals, hyenas, foxes, badgers, along with mongooses and jungle cats (the last named in the reeds along the Jordan River). Gazelles and other antelopes are common in the desert. Until fairly recent times the lion and the leopard stalked their prey on Jordanian soil, but these great cats are now extinct there.

A curious creature is the hyrax, small in size, resembling a rodent, but it has hoofs, can climb, and is considered by zoologists to be more closely allied to elephants than to any other animal group.

Birds are numerous, including quails, swans, cranes and cuckoos. The brown-necked raven is a characteristic bird of the Jordan Valley and the Palestine sunbird is typical of the Dead Sea area. Because of the dry climate, water-loving amphibians are few, but reptiles abound, including many species of snakes and lizards. Insects and their kin are very numerous in the dry regions, especially scorpions and locusts (which have attacked crops since Biblical days).

AMMAN

Long before recorded history, primitive people dwelt among the hills of Amman, enjoying the cool waters of its many springs. Instruments of flint have established their presence from Paleolithic times. Amman, later known as Philadelphia, was known in 1200 B.C. as Rabbath Amman, having been the capital of the Ammonites who fought with the biblical Kings of Israel.

Amman today is a modern city and among the fastest growing of national capitals. Its population has increased from 20,000 in 1920 to 500,000 today. Amman is famous for its 7 hills, its hotels, good food, archeological sites and friendly people.

Glimpses of ancient times linger in the long, winding bazaars where just about everything is sold. The bazaars contrast with shops and boutiques of ultra-fashionable design. Historic sites rival those of Europe—among the most impressive is the 2,000-year-old Roman Theatre

The Roman Theatre in Amman has a seating capacity of 6,000, and is still in use for festivals, concerts and other events.

The pool at the Philadelphia Hotel in Amman is a popular spot on a warm day.

Business as usual goes on in Amman's busy streets, in spite of the upheavals and privations caused by the tense situation in the Middle East.

facing a well-known tourist hotel, the Philadelphia. Guests at this hostelry are aware that a few steps away lies a trip back into time. The theatre, built in three tiers into the semi-circular curve of a hill, seats 6,000 spectators and is used today for outdoor festivals and orchestral concerts.

Other antiquities include the Citadel and its fine museum containing relics of the city's ancient history. On a hill just outside of Amman are the remains of a Roman temple to Hercules, a Byzantine Church and an Ommayyad palace from the 8th century A.D.

Development in the capital has exceeded expectations. Amman has a fine race track where camel racing is enjoyed as much as horse racing. Tennis clubs, swimming and glider clubs exist, while entertainment at the various hotels headlines performers of international reputation.

Several years ago Jordan's modern university opened its doors in the environs of Amman. Buildings of note are the two palaces where King Hussein lives and works. The Basman, a stately edifice, houses the royal offices—here the Parliament is opened and the King receives visitors, confers with his cabinet and more often than not stays late to complete the countless tasks always awaiting him. He dwells at the Ragadan Palace, the original Hashemite residence in Amman, where Hussein's grandfather, Abdullah, lived as Jordan's first ruler. Abdullah's tomb, a magnificent triple-arched shrine, is behind this palace. The main street of

Camel racing as a sport attracts enthusiastic crowds to the race track at Marka, just outside Amman.

Amman is King Hussein Street, in the heart of the city, a busy thoroughfare lined with modern buildings.

Modern Amman has fine hospitals and clinics, modern cinemas and an increasing number of factories producing cement, electrical apparatus, textiles, paper products and aluminium utensils. Food and tobacco-processing are among its most important industries.

Participants in a camel race enter the track at Marka. Racing camels are a special type—slender, light and fast.

This ancient double gate survives from the days when Amman was a walled city.

The graceful minaret of the Hussein Mosque towers over the heart of Amman.

JERASH

Known as the "Pompeii of the East," Jerash (in ancient times called Gerasa) is a 45-minute drive from Amman. Once it was a great city under Roman jurisdiction in the 2nd and 3rd centuries A.D., but later it decayed. The Jordan Department of Antiquities has dug it out of centuries of sand and debris, revealing hundreds of stately columns, a triumphal arch and other splendid ruins. Jerash was one of the renowned stops on the ancient caravan routes. All the treasures of the Orient found a market

Roman steps and columns (1st and 2nd centuries A.D.) lead up to the site of the early Christian cathedral at Jerash (4th century). At the top of the stairs is a shrine dedicated to the Virgin Mary and the archangels Gabriel and Michael.

The Nymphaeum, or Temple of the Nymphs, at Jerash was a sort of public fountain and temple combined. Water gushed out of holes in the lower niches into a tank. It dates from A.D. *190.*

here. Silks, spices and precious stones used as barter brought immense wealth to its citizens.

Jerash was the epitome of luxury in its day and Roman generals and wealthy townspeople enjoyed a life filled with expensive pleasures.

In the 2nd century A.D. Jerash entered its golden age. New buildings and lavish architecture were the order of the hour and Jerash attained the rank of an independent colony in the 3rd century. It only declined when the

The columns of Jerash rise spectacularly from the arid plain.

The forum at Jerash (seen here) stood at the end of a mile-long colonnaded street. Archeologists now believe that Jerash was far larger than at first supposed.

Romans themselves declined. Earthquakes in the 8th century hastened its end, and by the 13th century, the sands of the desert had swept across it and the ruined city was no more. Arabs passing through spoke of it as the "ruins of Jerash." Only a humble Arab village remained in our time when excavations and reconstruction began.

The paving blocks of the Roman Forum at Jerash are still in excellent condition.

A mosaic picture map of Jerusalem in the 6th century A.D. is one of the attractions of Madaba. The inscriptions are in Greek characters. Madaba was first mentioned in the Bible, in Numbers 21, as an Amorite town that was seized by the Moabites.

HADRIAN'S ARCH

The Roman Emperor Hadrian wintered in Jerash in A.D. 129–30, while making plans on a grand scale for the town. He built his own triumphal arch far away on the outskirts leaving part unfinished, suggesting that he meant the finished town walls to meet at his arch.

MADABA

Madaba lies just a 30-minute drive from Amman on rising ground in the middle of a plain where many battles were fought. An Ammonite town, it dates from the Middle Bronze Age and is noted for its Byzantine mosaics. One of the highlights is a 6th-century mosaic map of Jerusalem, the oldest map of the Holy City in the world. Embellished with mosaic pictures of monasteries, people, boats and plants, the map is preserved in the Greek Orthodox Church of Madaba. Other fine mosaics have been transferred to Madaba's small museum, where one can see depictions of Greek hero Achilles, the goatlike god Pan, and Bacchus the god of wine, along with exhibits of Roman jewels and utensils.

Madaba is just east of Mount Nebo, from the top of which Moses had his first view of the Promised Land. From this peak one can see the Jordan Valley and the Dead Sea, and on a clear day it is possible to see the spires of Jerusalem in the distance. Madaba reached its heights between the 5th and 6th centuries A.D. It was destroyed by the Persians in A.D. 614. Then it was occupied by the Arabs. In 747, an earthquake caused it to be abandoned until the early 19th century, when 2,000 Christians from Kerak settled there.

The vast Crusader castle at Kerak stands on a towering height above the Dead Sea. It was the southernmost fortress of the Crusader dynasty that ruled Jordan in the 12th century.

KERAK

Over the Mountains of Moab from Madaba lies the town of Kerak, a Crusader outpost of the 12th century. Its castle-fortress, one of the most renowned in all the Middle East, was built by the Crusader leader, Godfrey of Bouillon. Kerak lay across the trade routes that led from Arabia to Egypt and the Mediterranean. Stripping the caravans laden with brocades, ivory, spices, metals and jewels became a vital source of income for the Crusader military outposts. Saladin, the Saracen or Moslem leader, made numerous attempts to storm the castle, finally succeeding after starving out the defending Crusaders and took the great fortress in A.D. 1188.

Tales of Arab chivalry still remembered took place at Kerak. During the wedding feast of Humphrey of Toron, a Crusader knight and Isabel, sister of Baldwin, Saladin attacked the castle. The mother of the groom sent a gift of meat and wine with a message informing Saladin of the wedding. He replied, thanking her for the gift, while asking which tower was the bridal suite so that his soldiers would refrain from attacking it.

Kerak became an important and prosperous place in the later Middle Ages. When the Turks conquered the Middle East, they restored the castle, and, in spite of later neglect, it is still a historic and majestic sight, set in beautiful surroundings.

19

High above the valley floor at Petra are the ruins of cave dwellings.

The Siq is the narrow, winding passage through towering cliffs that leads to ancient Petra.

PETRA

This stronghold of an early people, the Nabataeans, is truly the chief attraction of Jordan. Petra was part of a forgotten past until it was discovered by a Swiss explorer, Burckhardt. He brought it to light in 1812, after hearing tales from guides about the ruins of an old city lost in the mountains. He induced the guides to take him there, by telling them of a sacrifice he was pledged to make at the reputed tomb of Abraham, which lay beyond Petra.

So bewildering was the glory of what he beheld—a noble city carved out of the mountain rock, statues from the Roman and Hellenistic eras, spacious cave dwellings half in

This huge finial ornament tops off one of Petra's largest monuments. Visitors are often challenged to climb it.

The Treasury is one of the finest of the amazing buildings at Petra. Note tiny horsemen in foreground.

The cave dwellings at Petra can still be used—some are inhabited by Bedouins today.

ruins, everything cut out of sandstone—that he was overcome. After he proclaimed his discovery, archeologists from all over the world flocked to it and were amazed at the grandeur and wealth of the still livable edifices. They recognized an art, a craftsmanship and a miracle of planning rarely achieved. The rough roads and rugged transport of those days deterred travellers, but today Petra, easily accessible over excellent roads, is but a 4-hour ride from Amman by car via Wadi-Musa's Police Post (reminiscent of the French Foreign Legion). Horses are obtained here for the fantastic narrow passage leading to the lost city, though jeeps can get through part of the way. The passage is an adventure in itself, for towering mountain walls block out the light and the sudden burst of daylight is blinding as one emerges from the Siq (which is the name of the passage) and beholds Petra.

The soft hues of the rock formations of Petra have given it the name of the "Rose red city, half as old as time." Many of its great tombs and caves are now occupied by Bedouin families. The softness of the sandstone did not allow for detailed sculpture, so the Nabataean artisans

Jordanians entertain tourists inside one of Petra's caves.

At Petra, a narrow stairway hewn out of solid rock leads to a flattened mountain top. Here is a huge altar of smoothed rock, called the "High Place," where pre-Christian Nabataeans made sacrifices.

devised a different method, a wider and more flowing style, reflected in the carved façades. The Place of Sacrifice, where religious ceremonies were performed and prisoners were sacrificed, is well preserved, and the Halls of Justice and the Monastery are giants of architectural beauty.

The Urn Temple at Petra was used by a Nabataean cult of the dead. Note the people at the right.

Grim hills devoid of vegetation overlook the boom port town of Aqaba.

The Water Ski Festival at Aqaba takes place against a background of purple mountains.

At Aqaba, the resort area is totally separate from the busy port.

AQABA

The road to lively Aqaba is the road to the Red Sea, since the city is situated on the Gulf of Aqaba. Aqaba is Jordan's only seaport, set against the rugged background of stark mountains, but the city itself is a scene of golden beaches, blue waters and flowers everywhere. At first sight, it appears to be mainly a tourist spot, for happy youngsters crowd the waterfront, bathers relax on the fine, warm sands, sailboats skim back and forth and all water sports seem to be the order of the day.

Aqaba was a place of importance long before water skis and scuba diving arrived, long before it became known as a winter resort, or famous for its Water Festival. Aqaba is the Hashemite Kingdom's outlet to the outside world of international trade. Its history can be traced back to King Solomon, when ore from the copper mines of the region was smelted in furnaces which took advantage of the winds always blowing from the north to keep their fires hot. Commerce flourished with Egypt and the small town had a busy life.

The city came into importance again in the later Middle Ages under the Mamelukes, whose last Sultan's name is still engraved on the town's ancient gateway, the Sultan Qansah el Ghuri.

Before the new docks for large vessels were built at Aqaba, passengers had to wait to be taken by launch back to their steamer at anchor in the bay.

The pink sands and black hills of Wadi Rumm sheltered the English adventurer, Lawrence of Arabia, and his Bedouin allies and served as the base from which they raided the Turkish outposts in World War I.

WADI RUMM

Wadi Rumm, the Valley of the Moon, between Petra and Aqaba is Lawrence of Arabia country. Among the deep sandstone cliffs of the Valley the British adventurer, Lawrence, helped the Arabs in the desert fight against the Turks in 1917. The mountains here are black, standing upon pale pink sands, and here falconry is still practiced by the Bedouins. The falcons are trained for months on end, and later are sold to the wealthy princes of Saudi Arabia.

The new highway to Wadi Rumm ends at the entrance to the Valley and is replaced by a primitive road which jeeps and camels can traverse with ease. Sweeping vistas provide miles and miles of scenery so breathtaking

that one feels humble among the immense plateaus partly covered with green desert scrub, where the mountains are overwhelmingly beautiful in the haze of the day and awesome in the clear blue night. In this landscape the filming of *Lawrence of Arabia* took place.

Large boulders here and there bear inscriptions centuries old. Bedouins on camels and young boys herding long-haired black goats are part of the scenery, as are the glimmering camp fires of travellers. Tourists can now enjoy desert camping at Wadi Rumm and the delights of food cooked over open fires by Bedouin guides, who know where to find overhanging rocks in the shade and gushing streamlets to quench thirst. A grand finale awaits campers at the Camel Corps Police Fort, where the Desert Legionnaires receive

Tourists at Wadi Rumm enjoy an open-air meal.

visitors with traditional black coffee, filling up the cups until everyone is satiated.

OTHER TOWNS

At Ajlun, the Castle of Saladin stands on the highest ground, at whose foot sprout luscious pomegranate trees and groves of figs. Pine and oak forests line the way to Ajlun, where Jordanians trek to enjoy picnics on a day's outing and a view of the Jordan Valley.

On the Jerash Road, north of Ajlun, lies the large commercial city of Irbid, near which is a mound covering the remains of a village dating back to 3,000 B.C.

About 30 miles (48 km.) north of Irbid, in the valley of the Yarmuk River, are hot sulphur springs, used for health baths. Many tourists visit here and residential and bathing facilities are set in an attractive background.

The old cities of the West Bank, under Israeli administration since 1967, include Bethlehem, Jericho, Nablus and Hebron.

Bethlehem and its famous Church of the Nativity were under Jordanian rule until 1967. A Christian Arab woman is kissing a silver star set in the floor of the grotto beneath the church.

27

Heavily fortified, Kharana Castle was built by the Ommayyads mainly to protect their caravan routes, although like all their castles, it was luxuriously appointed inside.

VILLAGES

The villages of Jordan range from those with 50 to 100 inhabitants to large ones with up to several thousands. The average Jordanian village is a compact settlement with houses close together, each built of stone with a courtyard surrounding it. In the smaller villages the dwellings are of one storey, and made of mud brick.

Castle Amra is the best preserved of the Ommayyad desert retreats.

A pierced stone window suggests the former luxury of the Hisham Winter Palace of the Ommayyads, dating from the 8th century.

DESERT CASTLES

A little known attraction of Jordan are the desert castles set amidst trees in the eastern part of the land, most of them used by the Ommayyad Caliphs around the 8th century A.D. Their main residence was in Damascus, but the Caliphs enjoyed life in the desert and would move with their entire entourage back to the land of their original Bedouin ancestry, to regain the pleasures of the simplicity and spaciousness of desert life.

The castles were created to house the Caliphs and their families and followers, and their concubines too. Dancing and music were the chief indoor amusements and vast pools, elaborately decorated with heating pipes, can still be seen, where the family spent hours relaxing between feasts and sports.

In the castle known as Kharana, 62 miles (99 km.) east of Amman, in the oasis of Azraq, are huge and mysterious basalt blocks and a mosque dating from the 13th century. Azraq now lies in the heart of a great National Park and reserve. Its enchanting oasis pools have yielded evidence of Paleolithic settlements, 200,000 years old.

Castle Amra, built in the early 8th century, 20 miles (33 km.) from Azraq, is considered the best preserved. Hunting scenes, figures of Victory, Philosophy, Poetry, even saluki dogs and Islam's enemies are shown on the numerous frescoes on the Castle's walls. Castle Mushatta, the nearest one to Amman, though covered with fine carvings and much delicate detail, was never completed. However, the gigantic remains reflect how ornate the Ommayyads' taste could be. Castle Hallabat, originally built in the reign of the Roman Emperor Caracalla (A.D. 198–217) as a fortress against raiding desert chiefs, is still well preserved.

Near Ajlun, Castle Qalat al Rabadh, a true Arab structure, has fortified double gates. Built by a governor of Saladin's near Ajlun to protect the Arabs from the Crusaders, it is not an Ommayyad Castle. Once it was part of a chain of bases and flying pigeon-posts that could flash news from the Euphrates to the Nile between dawn and dark. In 1927, the Department of Antiquities cleared its moats, gates and towers, and several deep wells inside the castle are in use today.

The Kidron Valley outside Jerusalem is one of the holy places which were under Jordan's control until 1967, and whose disposition remains to be settled. In the foreground, surrounded by terraced olive trees, is the Church of All Nations, which marks the spot where Jesus prayed before his arrest.

2. HISTORY

ANCIENT CONQUERORS marched across the land that is now Jordan, and each in turn left behind traces of their presence. From the east came Assyrians, Babylonians and Persians. Philistines, Hittites and Greeks appeared from the north and west. From the west also came the Romans and the Egyptians, and from the south finally came the Arabs, who stayed to make Jordan part of the Arab world.

Excavations at Jericho, in the disputed West Bank region, have shown remains of a civilization at least 8,000 years old.

Wadi Musa, near Petra, is a village on the site of a well which is believed to have been used by Moses.

EARLY HISTORY

Since ancient times, the huge deserts of the Arabian Peninsula have been the home of Semitic peoples. They were shepherds and, as their tribes grew larger and the deserts drier, they moved north in search of water for their flocks. Among them were the Canaanites, who reached the shores of the Mediterranean. All along the coastline and in the Jordan Valley, they built small cities.

The movement from the Arabian Peninsula during the Bronze and Middle Bronze Ages also included the Ammonites, Amorites, Moabites and Edomites, all familiar to readers of the Bible as ancient enemies of yet another Semitic people—the Israelites.

ISRAELITES

The Patriarch Abraham pitched his tribal tents at Hebron in the land of Canaan, where he and his family prospered. Later on there was famine in Canaan and the descendants of Abraham struggled to reach Egypt about 1700 B.C. At that time, Egypt was under the rule of desert invaders, the Shepherd Kings, or the Hyksos, who developed the war chariot.

About 1560 B.C. the Egyptians rebelled and regained control of their land, expelling the Hyksos. Moses, from the family of Abraham, emerged as a leader of the Israelites and led them from slavery in Egypt, across the Red Sea. For 40 years they wandered in the desert until Moses lay dying. His last act was to point out the rich Jordan Valley ahead of them. They crossed the Jordan, took Jericho and other Canaanite towns and established themselves in Palestine.

About 1000 B.C. David, one of the Children of Israel, became king, made great conquests and established Jerusalem as his capital. His son Solomon beautified Jerusalem and built the Temple there. In 586 B.C. Nebuchadnezzar, the Babylonian king, destroyed Jerusalem and took 50,000 Israelites into captivity in Babylon, where they remained until 538 B.C. when Cyrus of Persia captured Babylon and sent the Jews back to Jerusalem. In 333 B.C. Alexander the Great of Greece conquered Syria. Two hundred years later the Romans occupied Syria, Jordan and Palestine, and in the 1st century B.C. installed Herod the Edomite as King of the Jews. During Herod's reign, Jesus was born in Bethlehem.

The Monastery, one of Petra's most imposing structures, was built in the 3rd century A.D. as a pagan temple, and later was used as a Christian church.

NABATAEANS

The Nabataeans who first inhabited Petra amassed fortunes in the 5th century B.C., because their land lay close to the Syrian-Arabian border trade routes, and they collected large tolls from caravans for safe passage. They used their wealth to glorify their capital and named it Petra, which means "The Rock."

In later years the Nabataeans came under the Empire of Alexander the Great and his successors.

The Grecian Empire tumbled under pressure from Roman legions who tried in vain at first to capture Petra, though in the end its people had to pay tribute to Rome. In A.D. 107 Petra became part of the Roman Province of Syria. The Emperor Trajan built the first great road passing through Petra, connecting Syria with the Red Sea. Petra prospered beyond its dreams. As the Roman Empire declined, this route was abandoned in A.D. 300 and Petra lost much of its importance.

Christianity came to Petra in the next century but fewer caravans crossed its path. Decline set in and by the time of the Arab conquest in the 7th century, Petra was deserted.

PERSIAN OCCUPATION

About the year A.D. 600 the Persians won Syria and Palestine from the Eastern Roman or Byzantine Empire, which had acquired these territories through the break-up of the Roman Empire. In the end, in 614, they captured Jerusalem, massacred many of the people and pulled down all the Christian churches. The Persian occupation lasted less than 20 years until the Byzantine Emperor Heraclius came to Jerusalem, bringing with him several of the holy relics the Persians had taken away.

ISLAM

Islam, the religion of the Prophet Moham- med, was introduced into Jordan in the 7th century by Arab invaders. This happened after the Arabs, impelled by the new faith of Islam, swept out of the deserts of Arabia and defeated the Byzantine forces in A.D. 636. An era of peace and prosperity followed and Jerusalem's Famous Dome of the Rock (still standing today) was built by one of the Ommayyad Caliphs, Abdul Malak Ibn Marwan. Suc- cessors of Mohammed, the Caliphs were both spiritual and earthly leaders of the Arab realm. The Ommayyads, an Arab dynasty whose capital was Damascus, ruled from there for 100 years.

CRUSADERS

In A.D. 750, the Abbasids, a rival group, fought and conquered the Ommayyads, moving the Caliphate to Baghdad. They were unable to maintain control over Jordan and Palestine, which fell to the Frankish, or Western European, Crusaders. The aim of the Cru- saders was to restore the Holy Land to Christian rule. After Jerusalem fell into Crusader hands in 1099, following fierce warfare, the Crusaders built castles, north, west and south, to control the caravan routes, and also built thousands of churches and Christian shrines.

SALADIN

Once again Arab armies, those of Saladin and the Ayyubites, came to power and overthrew the Crusaders in 1187 in the Battle of Hittin near the Lake of Tiberias. The Ayyubite soldiers commanded the area until the Mame- lukes from Egypt took over. The Mameluke Sultans had aided in crushing the Crusaders and they now ruled in Jordan and Syria, forcing out all the Crusaders.

The interior of the Dome of the Rock in Jerusalem is richly ornamented in the Moslem style. One of the most holy shrines of Islam, this great mosque came under Israeli administration in 1967. Control of it is one of the many touchy problems still unresolved in the Arab-Israeli confrontation.

and ended in Medina, the Moslem pilgrimage city in Saudi Arabia. Turkish occupation of Jordan lasted until the end of World War I in 1918.

WORLD WAR I

As early as 1914, the Hashemites (direct descendants of the Prophet Mohammed) aspired to regain independence from Turkey. Sherif Hussein, a Hashemite who was Emir of Hejaz (the part of Arabia including the holy cities of Mecca and Medina), undertook the task of appealing to the Ottomans for self-rule. His appeal was in vain, and persecutions of the Arabs by the Turks resulted. Sherif Hussein, through his sons, contacted the Allies and an Arab revolt against the Turks was planned, to take place in 1916. Within 3 months after the revolt began, the Arab forces led by Hussein's sons forced a surrender from the Turkish garrisons with the exception of the one at Medina.

An independent Arab state was formed in Hejaz and Sherif Hussein was proclaimed King. After this event thousands of Arabs from other countries joined the Arab armies and fought on the side of the Allies, led by Emir Faisal, a son of Hussein, who captured Aqaba in July, 1917. This army also aided the British Army in Palestine by cutting off Turkish communications along the Hejaz Railway. Later all of Trans-Jordan (as it was then called) and Syria were conquered by the Arabs and British together.

FORMATION OF TRANS-JORDAN

Emir Faisal established an Arab government in October, 1918, at Damascus. Britain and France then declared their intention of dividing Syria, Palestine and Trans-Jordan into French and British spheres of influence. In July, 1920, French forces advanced from Lebanon, occupied Damascus and expelled Emir Faisal. Quarrelsome peace negotiations followed and two documents came to light which caused great shock to the Arabs.

Jordan's famous Arab Legion was trained by a legendary Englishman, General John Bagot Glubb, known as "Glubb Pasha." One of the results of his efforts is the unusual sight of a Jordanian soldier piping "Retreat" on a true Scottish bagpipe.

TURKISH DOMINATION

In the meantime, invaders from Central Asia had conquered much of the Middle East. One group, the Ottoman Turks, had occupied Anatolia and parts of Persia. By 1516, they had annexed Syria, Jordan and Palestine. The Ottoman Turks, although they had adopted Islam, reigned as cruel lords for 400 years. It was 400 years of hate, corruption and neglect. They seized power, collected taxes, imposed restrictions, denying the people health and medical care, and education. Jordan, Palestine and Syria were poverty stricken and their inhabitants lived like slaves. The only development of worth made by the Turks was the Hejaz Railway which ran from Turkey to Aleppo in Syria, over to Damascus, down to Amman

This water trough is fed by a spring which the Bedouins call "Lawrence's Well," after the English desert hero, who often camped near the spring.

SECRET AGREEMENTS

The first document was the Sykes-Picot Agreement made secretly in 1916 between the French and the British. The second document was the Balfour Declaration in which the British said they "looked with favour" upon the creation of a "national home for Jewish people" in Palestine.

This appeared to be unbelievable to the Arabs and a double blow to them. They discovered that they were not going to have complete Arab independence and learned that the Arab Middle East was to be divided, according to the Sykes-Picot Agreement into a French and a British Mandate.

Trans-Jordan had been administered by the Arab government in Damascus. In October, 1920, Emir Abdullah (another son of Hussein) arrived at Ma'an, a town in southern Jordan, at the head of an Arab force. In response to the wishes of the people of Trans-Jordan, the Emir entered Amman in March, 1921, and established an Arab government there.

THE NEW STATE

Britain did not wholly relinquish control of Trans-Jordan, however. A British resident, with a staff of British advisers, was installed in Amman and remained there until after World War II. During the war Trans-Jordan actively supported the Allies, through its army, the Arab Legion. Emir Abdullah was proclaimed King in 1946 and a new constitution replaced the old one. The country at long last had full sovereignty.

On May 15, 1948, Britain relinquished its mandate over Palestine and the new state of Israel was proclaimed, formed from parts of the mandate. Immediately the surrounding Arab states attacked the new nation. These countries were allied in the League of Arab States, formed in 1945, including Egypt, Syria, Lebanon, Iraq and Trans-Jordan.

After the cessation of hostilities between the Arabs and the Jews in Palestine in 1949, the Jordanian Parliament representing Central Arab Palestine and Trans-Jordan, approved the union of these two regions, forming one country. The new state was called "The Hashemite Kingdom of Jordan." Of the two regions, Palestine was then known as "West Bank" and the other, Trans-Jordan, became the "East Bank" of today. The holy city of Jerusalem was divided in two by the boundary between Israel and Jordan. The newly formed government of Jordan, at its first parliamentary session in 1951, drew up a constitution.

THE ASSASSINATION

In 1951, King Abdullah, on a visit to Jerusalem accompanied by his grandson, Prince Hussein, went for prayers to Aqsa Mosque. There he was assassinated, apparently by Arab terrorists, while the young prince was unharmed. The shock to Jordanians was so great, a crisis existed during which time Abdullah's son Talal was crowned King. Because of ill health, King Talal later abdicated and was succeeded by his son, Hussein, then 17 years old.

King Hussein, in military uniform, is ready to make a radio speech shortly after ascending the throne of Jordan.

The courage and informality of King Hussein (here at the wheel of one of his many cars) has won the support of the Jordanian people.

HUSSEIN'S REIGN

Three times, after Hussein ascended the throne, Egypt and Syria went to war with Israel—in 1956, 1967 and in 1973. In all these encounters, the Jordanian king managed to keep Jordanian participation to a minimum. Hussein's rule has been jeopardized by the presence of large numbers of Palestinian Arab refugees in the East Bank area of Jordan. His attempts to curtail their activities have brought him close to being assassinated more than once.

Palestinian Arab refugees wait outside a clinic in a refugee camp near Amman.

King Hussein and Crown Prince Hassan (second from right) join in a dance with enlisted men of the Jordanian Army.

3. GOVERNMENT

THE CONSTITUTION of the Hashemite Kingdom declares Jordan to be an hereditary monarchy under the King, who has powers over the legislative, executive and judicial branches.

THE KING

King Hussein, born in 1935, second son of King Talal, selected by his father to take his place while still a minor in 1952, formally ascended the throne of the Hashemite Kingdom in 1953.

Years later, King Hussein told about his grandfather's assassination in his biography. One could sense the sorrow in his remarks. The mental shock had prepared him for a possible similar attempt, and therefore he resolved to live his life to the fullest each day, knowing it could well be his last.

Apart from his courage the King is a sports enthusiast—he flies his own plane, is an amateur radio operator, enjoys miniature car racing and all forms of water sports. Like other fathers he takes his children on picnics, is

King Hussein is an enthusiastic pilot and usually flies his own plane.

Hussein chose his youngest brother, Prince Hassan, who was proclaimed Crown Prince of the Hashemite Kingdom on April 1st, 1965.

THE LEGISLATURE

The legislature is composed of two branches, both of whose members are notables of the Al-Ayan clan, selected by the Prime Minister, who in turn is chosen by the King, subject to parliamentary approval, as is the cabinet. The King wields final powers over the legislature, however. Elections for deputies are held every 4 years. Political parties are banned, but all men 18 years of age or older may vote, provided they meet certain legal standards; excepted are the men of the royal family. About 75 per cent of the eligible citizens vote.

The cabinet acts and supervises the work of the different sections of the government and establishes general policy. In the years previous to 1957 (when parties were banned), there were numerous political parties, including the Moslem Brotherhood, Communists, Arab Ba'th, Socialists, the Liberation Movement and the Community Party, but their membership was very limited.

proud of their efforts and will not allow them preferential treatment because they are of royal blood—they must earn their credits, prizes and high marks.

Though the monarchy is hereditary, the King may select whom he wishes for his heir, provided he is of the same royal blood.

Ladies of the royal family include (left) Princess Alia, only child of King Hussein's first marriage, Princess Basma (middle) and (right) his second wife, Princess Muna (from whom he is now divorced).

Crown Prince Hassan of Jordan (left) and his guest, the Crown Prince of Bahrain, drink orange juice at a meeting. Notice the engraved hilt of the golden sword, always worn tucked in a leather belt.

JUDICIARY

Judges for the judiciary are appointed (or dismissed) by royal decree and the judiciary is constitutionally independent of the other branches. There are three classes of courts. The first consists of regular courts, including magistrates courts, courts of the first instance and courts of appeals and cassation in Amman, which hear appeals from lower courts. The constitution provides for a Special Council which interprets laws and passes on their constitutionality.

The second category is made up of religious courts for both Moslems and non-Moslems; these have jurisdiction over matters of a personal nature such as marriage and divorce. The third category consists of special courts, such as land, government, property, municipal, custom and tax courts.

The Queen Mother, Queen Zein (left) is revered by Jordanians as the mother of their very popular King.

Camels of a desert patrol rest while Camel Corps police visit a Bedouin tent.

SOCIAL AND ECONOMIC POLICIES

Jordan is in the midst of a struggle for power in a whirling mass of Middle East problems, bounded by Israel, an enemy that would prefer to be a friend on the West, and by Syria and Iraq (who are not so friendly to Jordan) to the north and east. Within Jordan's own borders there are tensions and cliques and different ideologies (which exist throughout all Arab lands) and the struggle between them often erupts. The Jordanian government attempts at all times to foster loyalty and seeks to accelerate social changes. Schemes have been initiated to raise the standard of living, with better housing, free education for all and increased medical care. The government strives to offer alternatives to the leftist aims and theories that are just beginning to affect the Arab world. In spite of jealousies and constant intrigues, not to mention the influx of refugees, social improvements have proceeded in an uninterrupted manner.

GOVERNORATES

Jordan is divided into 8 administrative units called governorates, which in turn are divided into districts and sub-districts. The Minister of the Interior chooses a worthy official to head each governorate. Generally it is a local

At Amman's Roman Theatre a match is in progress between a Jordanian Army boxer and a member of a visiting group from the United States.

Another of the pilgrimage sites in the disputed West Bank region is the Mount of Temptations, near Jericho, where Christ is said to have fasted 40 days and 40 nights, after he was baptized in the Jordan. Halfway up the Mount, a Greek Orthodox monastery is built around the cave where he fasted.

citizen of high repute who has earned his position as "a son of the people." In this manner he is looked upon as a tribal father. His word is obeyed and his advice sought. In the cities, the mayor and his elected council take care of the local affairs. It is surprising to note that in the West Bank, despite the Israeli military occupation, the former municipal councils are almost all in operation, continuing their manner of administration as before.

THE ARMY

The most striking thing about Jordan's armed forces is that there is no conscription—no one is forced to join. Young Jordanians consider it a privilege to join. Many youngsters today from tender school ages join the army as reserves. Each of King Hussein's two young sons, at the age of 9, took two years of training, just like any Jordanian soldier (after school hours).

It is estimated that 60,000 soldiers serve in all branches of the armed forces of Jordan. The Air Force, though small, is equipped with modern jet aircraft, developed from the Arab Legion, originally taught by British officers. The King is Commander-in-Chief.

RELATIONS WITH ISRAEL

The Jordanian Government has never given up hope of regaining the West Bank and the pilgrimage places which attracted thousands of foreign visitors and provided financial gain. King Hussein has no peace plan to offer for their return. He relies on the United Nations and especially the United States for help in this direction.

Hussein's policy, both foreign and domestic, has been one of general solidarity with the Arab world. He has avoided friction with Israel, as shown by his action in suppressing the Palestinian guerrilla forces in his land. The Israeli occupation and the refugees pouring

between the East and West Banks, and discussions have been held with West Bank leaders relating to joint planning.

To the outside world, the occupied West Bank of the Hashemite Kingdom appears to be sealed off to Jordanians in the East Bank. In the beginning of the occupation, this was so. For quite some time now, all a Jordanian or any Arab residing in Jordan, as well as foreign residents, has to do is to apply for a permit to visit the West Bank and families and friends. It is as easy as buying a railway ticket and the results make for happiness on both sides of these man-made barriers.

OUTLOOK

into Jordan contributed to the rise of extremist Palestinian guerrilla organizations. The destruction by Israel of many communities on the East Bank by shelling and air attacks indeed led to the civil war in 1970 and 1971, in which Jordan's army expelled the guerrilla fighters with a great deal of bloodshed.

By mid-1974, the climate was healthier, with a feeling in Jordan of greater internal security and business confidence. There are even some business transactions going on

The challenges affecting the nation are still enormous. The Israeli war and its aftermath created social and economic furor. Subsequent events forced thousands of people living on the eastern side of the Jordan Valley to move to the highlands in order to seek protection from casual air and ground attacks from the Israelis. Jordan is determined to handle these disruptions by absorbing refugees and devoting greater efforts to normalize the daily life of its citizens within its borders.

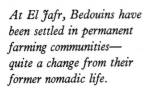

At El Jafr, Bedouins have been settled in permanent farming communities— quite a change from their former nomadic life.

Old and new are blended in this scene—a woman in Western dress still wears a veil, as she passes new shops being built in traditional Arab style.

4. THE PEOPLE

MOST OF THE 2,350,000 people of Jordan are Arabs, speaking Arabic. In addition to the classic Arabic written language, there are various dialects differentiated by local accents and inflections. About 12 per cent of the people are Christians, and the rest are Moslems. Besides the Arabs, there are small numbers of Circassians, Turcomans, Armenians, Kurds, White Russians and approximately 220 Samaritans, remnants of an ancient Jewish sect from Biblical times, who live in Nablus, on the West Bank. At least 200 Druzes live in and around Amman. The Bahai-Persians—about 200 of them—live in the Jordan Valley. The Circassians are a Sunni Moslem group numbering about 1,000, descendants of an immigrant group from the Caucasus. The Turcomans, a non-Arab community, inhabit the village of Rammun near Jerash.

These ethnic groups present a picturesque diversity in dress, related to the secular background.

Jordan is a country of youth—more than half the people are under the age of 19 years.

Bethlehem on the West Bank, now under Israeli control, was part of Jordan when these refugee children were photographed there.

REFUGEES

The influx of refugees has altered the population map of Jordan, affecting its social, political and business life. There were approximately 700,000 in 1966, and 350,000 more refugees arrived after the Arab-Israeli war of 1967. Many have since acquired Jordanian citizenship and make significant contributions to the country's welfare, having uplifted themselves out of the refugee camps. Thousands live in Jordan's 29 refugee camps, part of them in huts and tents, but a good number have small, sturdy houses within the camp areas. Schools,

Many of the refugees on the West Bank prior to 1967 lived in crude shelters such as this one at Hebron.

A tidy refugee camp adjoins well-tilled fields in the Baq'a Valley.

clinics and other health facilities are built around the camps. Teen-aged refugees are taught useful trades and the young girls specialize in fine needlework. Since the inhabitants of the camps by and large insist on returning eventually to their homes, they are classified as "displaced persons who resist efforts at resettlement." As such, they are supported by the United Nations Relief Agencies for Palestine Refugees in the Near East.

The largest of all refugee camps in Jordan is Aqabat Jaber, which houses 32,000 people, including these women going to and from a well. It is usual for the women to carry all types of vessels neatly balanced on their heads.

45

Bedouin tents are still a common sight in Jordan.

The male members of a Bedouin family are ready to receive visitors—the women remain out of sight.

Bedouin hosts instruct a guest from the city in the proper method of eating "manseh."

A Bedouin woman and her donkey stop at a waterhole at Q'a Disi.

BEDOUINS

The Bedouins of Jordan are among the most picturesque of all its people. Their home is the desert, stretching from Syria and Iraq in the north, to the dimly marked Saudi border in the south. Besides being crossed by ancient caravan routes the desert is dotted with oases and wells from Azraq to Wadi Rumm—here the Bedouin is still king.

There are three principal Bedouin tribes—the Beni Sakhrs, the Huywaytats and the Sirhans. Once they were all cattle drovers, but now some of them have added sheep and goats to their flocks. All three tribes share the traditions of desert life, which are chivalry, courage and hospitality.

They have the greatest reverence for King Hussein. In his biography, Hussein describes them:

This Bedouin at El Jafr owns a house now—but he prefers to live in a tent nearby with his sons, while his wife occupies the house.

Jordan's famous Camel Corps patrols the vast desert areas, aiding tourists and Bedouins alike.

"When I visit my tribes, I sit at the head of the tent with other guests around me. Members of the tribe stand in front, dancing their traditional dances and singing. When my name is mentioned in a song, they shoot their rifles in the air as a salute. After I sit down, coffee is served. Then the chief of the tribe makes his traditional welcome speech, composing it as he goes along. Soon a poet appears and makes up poetry as he talks.

"Then comes dinner—usually a *manseh* consisting of yellow rice and lamb cooked in large pots. Literally, manseh means a big dish, and sometimes a score of lambs will be slaughtered. We recline on silken cushions in tents 50 yards long. No women are allowed, and no members of the tribe—even the chief—eat until all the guests are finished."

This is hospitality, Bedouin style. The pattern of their lives varies according to the size of the tribe. Some tribes consist of only a few families, or of a father, the families of his sons and his unmarried daughters. Tribes like the Beni Sakhr often have 2,000 to 3,000 interrelated families, all of whom owe family allegiance to the tribal *sheikh*, the ruling head of the family. In such a tribe there may be as many as a dozen sheikhs.

For the entertainment of guests there is, camel racing, while the food is being prepared.

The meal is served buffet style, with neither plates nor cutlery. Desert protocol demands that all eat from the same dish, with the right hand. Before the meal and between courses, bowls of warm water and soap and towels are passed round so that each person has clean fingers for the repast.

King Hussein is never too busy to receive a Bedouin visitor.

CITY LIFE

In contrast to the life of the desert people, the city folk of Amman are on the whole a well educated crowd; cosmopolitan in approach, friendly to strangers and dressed in Western style. Balls and concerts are often held in Amman for the purpose of benefiting some public causes—and King Hussein may donate a car or some other expensive object as a drawing card to attract more participants. In this manner a new Fine Arts building has come into being in Amman.

The King himself is often seen in public in Amman. Passing alone in his jeep through the city some years ago, he noticed a street demonstration and flare-up. The Army had been sent for to maintain order, but Hussein drove into the disturbance, walked out of his jeep, strode in the midst of the fray and casually conversed with the angry crowd. In minutes all was peaceful and citizens were shaking hands not only with His Majesty but with each other. This is the spell of Hussein, reputed to be the most unafraid person in the Hashemite Kingdom.

A confectioner makes fresh sweets in the "souk" at Amman—he always offers his customers a taste before they make a purchase.

THE SOUK TRADERS

A different world exists in the bazaars, or *souks*, of Jordan. Peopled by shrewd but friendly merchants who own every kind of goods, the bazaars have a jovial air, yet serious business is carried on (with hourly tea and coffee breaks). A tourist is coddled—the customer has refreshments on the house, no matter whether he is local or foreign. In the jewel sections, one sees craftsmen ply their trade and wait on ladies with great gallantry. The *souks* have an Arabian Nights air, out of another era, seldom changing and extremely picturesque.

Women in traditional dress proceed cautiously over the mud along the banks of the Seil, a narrow drainage channel running through Amman. The Seil was being provided with a concrete cover when this photograph was taken in 1969.

These wary-looking Bedouin schoolboys are just getting used to settled life in a new village.

EDUCATION

The modernization taking place in Jordan requires a high standard of education. No longer does family and social status determine the future of aspiring youth. Jordan has not yet become a society where people of all backgrounds can advance on their merits alone—yet many leadership positions cannot be maintained without specialized education. For most Jordanians, education has become a status symbol and a true source of social prestige.

The expansion of educational opportunities at all levels has led to great changes. Many children from the poorest families have been able to become university graduates, doctors, scientists and engineers. This came to pass because of the system of free education at all levels—elementary, preparatory and secondary education—with scholarships offered to those who show promise. In the new life-style of Jordan, education has become top priority and schools are now found in the most remote stretches of the southern and eastern part of the country, desert areas included.

Education is compulsory for all children. Books are free and about 70 per cent of Jordan's children now go to the government schools.

Villagers who were traditionally against education for girls no longer object to the fact that their daughters have to sit in co-educational village schools in one classroom. This is due to the achievements of the government as well as the participation and new interest of parents who have come to realize the immense value of education as the best way to fulfilment.

Indeed, village fathers tell future grooms: "My daughter can do more than sew and cook. She is a scholar, she reads and writes and is an asset to you and your farm. With her education, no one can cheat you." This makes the young man take notice. He accepts less dowry and secretly attends night classes to improve his own status. Love and a well stocked farm are no longer sufficient. He has to match her in brain power before her father allows him to accept her hand in marriage.

The Ministry of Education not only runs the schools, it establishes the curriculum, and sets the state examinations throughout the system, which calls for 6 years of elementary and 3 years of secondary studies. Young Jordanians seeking higher education attend the University in Amman. The University started with but one faculty in 1962. Since then, five faculties have been added. These are the Faculties of

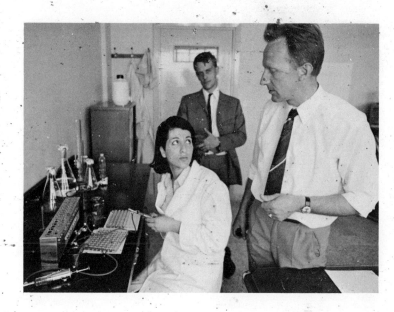

United Nations livestock experts work with a Jordanian woman laboratory assistant in examining samples of chicken blood.

Science, Economics and Commerce, Medicine and Islamic Law. From an original enrolment of 167 men and 18 young ladies, the student body had grown to 2,076 by mid-1974. New buildings are under construction for postgraduate study in social sciences, geology and antiquities, as well as a mosque and another library.

COLLEGE OF SHARIAH

This is the new faculty of Islamic Law. It is unusual, for no system exists to prepare clerics in Islam. A student must truly want to be a teacher, a preacher or a religious judge in Islam. Formerly young Jordanians had to go to Egypt and live and study at the Al Azhar University of Islamic studies in Cairo. The Government aimed to keep Jordanian youth at home, by creating the Shariah, where education and living expenses are given free. There are opportunities for immediate assignments upon completion of the 4-year course, which confers a bachelor's degree in religion. Some graduates become judges in Islamic courts of law, others will be speakers and preachers in the mosques.

OTHER SCHOOLS

Other educational facilities are the Banking Institute, the Television and Audio-Visual Apparatus Centre, and the School Health Divisions and Teacher Training Colleges. There are also private schools and missionary schools. Always crowded is the Agricultural Training Institute, where the students, many of whose forefathers were farmers who considered school-learning a waste of time, now absorb all the knowledge they can.

A large number of vocational schools including nursing and military institutes exist besides private and missionary schools. The impact of the 1967 war curtailed new projects that had commenced for children on the West Bank and in Jerusalem.

LIBRARIES

In Amman there are many libraries filled with books in Arabic, English and other languages. The American Embassy has a fine library open to the public, with current American magazines as well as books for pleasure or study. Other embassies have small libraries filled with literature in their own language.

51

Arab Christians present a folk dance during a Christmas celebration.

abundant as in former years. However, there is a great deal of Islamic decoration in architectural design, though it is mixed with the artisans' desire for today's modernity.

FESTIVALS

In the big cities, as well as in the villages, weddings call for dances and a festival which lasts for days on end. There are special songs for all occasions—for births, funerals, weddings, circumcisions, sowing, planting, plowing and harvesting. The festivals for harvesting are traditional rituals. Jordanians would not harvest without them and all the family, along with relatives, take part. Many dances begin with the pounding of feet on the floor to mark the rhythm—this is called the *debkah*. The dance known as the Sahjeh is the one performed by the Bedouins, while the Circassians have their own sword dance. Like the gypsies, the Circassians create dances to match their mood. The government has formed a national Circassian troupe that goes from town to town and also appears on television, while their songs are played on the radio.

CULTURE

Jordan's most famous writer is the late Mustafa Wabbah at-Tal, whose poetry ranks him among the most important Arab poets of the 20th century. Government efforts have been directed toward promoting the arts, under the guidance of the Ministry of Culture and Information. A fine art gallery is open every day in Amman and there is an archeological museum there, also. Due to strong Western influence, traditional Islamic art is not as

A girl in elaborate costume performs the "debkah," Jordan's most popular folk dance.

When the desert patrol comes to call upon the Sheikh of the local Bedouin tribe, it is a highly ritualized occasion. While sheep are killed and cooked, the guests are entertained with camel races. When the meat and rice are done, everyone is seated on layers of spread blankets under the tent, and the huge trays of meat and rice or "mansehs" are brought in, hot and highly seasoned.

FOOD

Jordanian cuisine is hearty and satisfying. Many Western-style restaurants have opened in recent years, featuring American and European specialities, but they also proudly feature Jordanian dishes. In Aqaba, fish dishes are popular—charcoal-broiled, highly seasoned —especially shrimp and lobster caught in the Red Sea. Jordanians enjoy *manseh*, which is a dish of lamb, sweet peas and yellow-gold rice, cooked long and simmered well. Food is never undercooked in Jordan, but is always well done.

Dinner in a prosperous Jordanian home may begin with appetizers, such as small shish-kebabs, roasted sardines and tiny meat balls, accompanied by conversation. The meal itself starts with a spicy cup of soup, a combination of lamb broth and onions with green peppers. This may be followed by *manseh* or by thick chick peas or quite often roast lamb. The dessert may be anything from a chocolate pudding, a very sweet coconut dish, or a flan, followed by fresh fruit and thick, dark, pungent Bedouin coffee, without which a meal is never complete.

The Jordanians enjoy beer—they toss down olives and nuts with it any time of the day. Jordanians delight in cold drinks. Small clay barrels hold home-made fruit concoctions, sold in stalls in every city and hamlet. These beverages are made from papaya, sugar cane, pineapple, oranges and lemons. Between the beer and the fruit drinks, one never goes thirsty in Jordan.

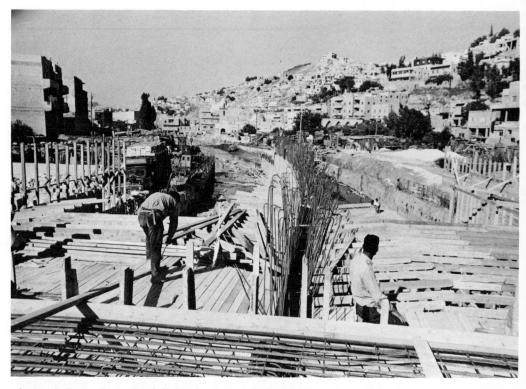

Acres of slums along the Seil in the heart of Amman have been cleared to make way for new construction. Here the Seil is in the process of being roofed over.

HEALTH AND WELFARE

In former times, health and welfare services were dispensed by private organizations. It was only in 1951 that a Ministry of Social Affairs was established in Jordan, which now supervises 350 social and charitable organizations, and administers welfare projects.

Infectious diseases have been brought under control and a national health insurance plan covering medical, dental and eye care is available at a very modest cost. Those who cannot afford it are treated free. Excellent hospitals and clinics exist in Amman and all the larger cities. The villages are supplied with rural medical services and visiting nurses.

The Ministry of Health has upgraded an old school of nursing into a college to train nurses. Instruction is in English, although the students must be Jordanian citizens between 17 and

The new town of Jebel is one of many communities built in recent years in the Amman metropolitan area.

Not a swimming pool, this is a small reservoir in the middle of new housing at El Jafr.

25 years of age. They are offered free tuition and all maintenance, plus a comfortable stipend. After graduation, they work for the Ministry as visiting nurses. The Ministry of Defence has a similar institution whose graduates work in the hospitals of the Jordanian Army. There are also medical clinics in all the refugee camps.

The Social Ministry trains young men and women for family care, social work, child care and community and individual welfare. The social development of the country is furthered by the Jordan Institute of Social Work, where specialists are trained in research, general economics, social statistics and social surveys.

HOUSING

Housing in Jordan is still inadequate, even though new construction goes on without interruption. In the 1960's many families were found to be living in one room. Even today, most of the newer dwellings are available for people in the middle-income range.

The Housing Corporation, established in 1965, is trying to alleviate this problem, knowing that about 14,000 houses for the very low-income groups must be under construction each year. So far about 6,000 houses annually have been completed, a step in the right direction for the working class.

Not all of Jordan's reservoirs are new—north of Jerash are Roman pools built 20 centuries ago over springs, to provide water for the city.

The Palace of Culture is one of the main structures at Hussein Youth City.

HUSSEIN YOUTH CITY

King Hussein envisioned this vast complex when he proposed this city within a city as a meeting place for youth of all ages, hoping that eventually it will attract the Olympic Games to Amman. Located just outside Amman, Hussein Youth City today embraces activities such as exhibitions, concerts, lectures and all types of athletics. It was completed in 1972 after 8 years of intense and careful construction.

Built to exacting international standards, with the Jordanian government donating 94.3 acres (37.7 hectares) of land, the Youth City grew with the help of donations from the people. Schools, scouts and the general public raised money for its inception with the help of a committee appointed by the King. Construction was handled by Jordanian firms who used mostly fine Jordanian tiles, marble, cement and asphalt, following the plans of British architects.

The seating section holds 2,500 spectators. Green and red marble walls reflect the hues of the country's flag. The cultural building with theatre, press, radio and conference rooms is an impressive sight, while the football field has a carpet of grass and extensive illumination for night sports. The swimming pools meet Olympic standards, and there are even small ones for small children. Lunch spots range from grandiose to cafeterias. Surrounding this vast complex are 30,000 trees.

With United Nations aid, the Baq'a Valley is being turned into irrigated fields like these.

5. ECONOMY

THE HASHEMITE Kingdom's chief natural resources are land and water, and therefore it is only natural that its major economic activity is agriculture and at least one third of the active population takes part in it. However, Jordanian agriculture in part is unstable because a large proportion of the total agricultural output comes from dry farming in areas which have numerous droughts. Special emphasis has been given in the past and in the present to irrigation schemes, soil and water projects which have raised quotas of drought-resistant crops in areas where irrigation is not possible.

AGRICULTURE

Steady improvement and increased cultivation have rewarded the Ministry of Agriculture's efforts. Annual fruit and vegetable production has risen from an average of 196,000 tons (176,400 tonnes) in the 1950's to above 550,000 tons (495,000 tonnes), with tomatoes and eggplants in the lead. Melons, cabbages, cucumbers and rice are the most popular food for Jordanians, and olives and nuts are also major crops. The country has attained self-sufficiency in most of its produce, and even exports large quantities to other countries.

MINING

Jordan's most important minerals are phosphates and limestone (for cement). Since the Dead Sea contains many dissolved minerals, the recovery of potash and magnesium is carried on. Clays, copper ore and silica are plentiful. Other minerals of commercial value to the land are manganese and oil shale.

Mother-of-pearl is found in large quantities in the Gulf of Aqaba, and is made up into beautiful necklaces and decorative religious objects. Marble abounds in Jordan and ranks high among its exports, along with the mother-

Jordan's economic development plans call for increased export of products derived from Jordanian minerals. Here a government exploration team searches for clay suitable for pottery manufacture.

of-pearl. The phosphate deposits contribute a great deal to the economy by their export. At least 6,000 persons are employed in the mining and quarrying fields.

FISHERIES

Current plans include adding to the fisheries in Aqaba and the factory for processing fish meal and other fish products. The once small fishing village by the side of the Red Sea is to be transformed into a hub of both business and tourism.

INDUSTRY

Industrial activity is diversified and has emerged as a rapidly growing force. Local materials are now being utilized to produce light consumer goods, such as canned fruits and vegetables, cigarettes, pure olive oil, vegetable fats, batteries, underwear, shirts and other light items of everyday use.

There are cement, paper and pharmaceutical factories, plus several marble works, employing thousands of Jordanians. Some of the many

foundries, the tannery and an enlarged phosphate plant have day and night shifts. Further full-time industrial activities include milling, oil pressing, bottling and brewing, tobacco products, footwear, metal production, furniture, glass printing and canning of Jordan's famous cashew nuts and Jordan almonds. Recently King Hussein opened a textile factory which operates on a 24-hour basis. The designs show a craftsmanship that is said to equal the textiles from New York, Paris and London.

HANDICRAFTS

The artisans of Jordan today use techniques that blend methods as old as the Bronze Age and as new as power-driven drills. Reflecting the long influence of Islam (which forbids representations of the human body), designs used in carving, metal work and embroidery are mainly plant, flower, animal and geometrical motifs. Reflecting Christian traditions, other designs portray crosses and images of saints. A popular theme is Saint George and the Dragon. Proverbs engraved in Arabic and

Built on Jebel Ashriyeh, one of the 7 hills of Amman, this new mosque is adorned with the brilliant tiles for which Jordanian architecture is famous.

English in delicate lettering are usually part of the design.

The carved wood industry is flourishing—its products are purchased by tourists and local people. Most of the carvings are made from Jordan's own olive trees, with the strong grain showing as part of the figure and design. The artisans wait a whole year for the olive wood to dry and harden. The finished objects are polished off by hand rubbing with beeswax, varnish or plastic coating. Imported wood of other types is used to make furniture.

Metal work, such as costume jewelry with religious motifs very beautifully done, is largely silver. However, wrought iron furniture is used a lot, and goldsmiths can be seen sitting outside their shops and stalls in the bazaars working in the daylight, using techniques handed down from father to son. Their specialities are Crusader Crosses and Islamic symbols. Bronze work is also done to adorn churches and houses.

Mother-of-pearl is obtained in Aqaba, where refugees from Bethlehem make boxes, necklaces, prayer beads and countless fine objects which have achieved world fame. Embroidery too (done by young girls who learn it from their mothers) is much in demand by tourists in the form of tablecloths and other domestic items.

TOYS

Toys have become a new important industry. Extremely attractive are the painted and handmade dolls in regional costumes. Earthenware toys found in excavations have been copied by factories which now turn out large quantities. Toys are also made from raffia. Shopping and laundry baskets more handsome than those found in Europe or America are inexpensive in Jordan. Table mats and wastepaper baskets are produced by the thousands in local factories.

MOSAICS

Village dwellings and modern homes traditionally have some mosaic work on walls and floors, as well as mosaic objects of art. All kinds of trinkets are made in mosaic and some are formed into bracelets, earrings and brooches. Cloisonné enamel work is also done by native artisans.

CARPETS

Most carpets for local trade are made of sheepskin and are the kind which the Bedouins use to cover the ground in their tents. The Bedouin can wash his rug, as it is very strong, does not fade and lasts for years. Villagers make many rugs in bright wools. Goat and camel threads are used, tinted in many hues. In Kerak and Shaubak (hubs of rug making), the designs are more Western.

THE WORK FORCE

Early in the 20th century, Jordanian women did not go out to business or work. Even the domestics were men, since strict Moslems do not permit their wives to be seen by other men with the exception of relatives. Therefore, women could not go to work and mix with

At Aqaba, conveyor belt installations can load phosphates at the rate of 500 tons (550 metric tons) an hour.

strange people. Jordan has since become far more modern and 20 per cent of workers are women in factories. In the cities, elegant young Jordanian women work as secretaries, in public relations jobs, in the television and radio stations and as clerks and saleswomen. Some of the leading families have boutiques run by their womenfolk. Many a lady, widowed or divorced, has surmounted her problems by opening a business dedicated to what she excels in.

The real work force, however, is the male population and the economically active workers number about 540,000. Many operate their own shops with the help of relatives.

TRADE AND FINANCE

Jordan has special laws designed to encourage and promote development by foreign investment, by offering tax exemptions and many facilities. The Industrial Development Corporation studies projects and prospective offerings. The Industrial Development Bank, a joint venture between private and public sectors, established in 1965, provides credit for industrial projects. By 1972, it had extended loans totalling 3,500,000 Jordanian dinars. The Jordanian currency, the dinar, is equal approximately to the British pound sterling.

The Three Year Development Plan (1973-75) aims at expanding trade by opening up new markets. Jordan is one of the founding members of the Council for Arab Economic Unity and the Arab Common Market. Trade agreements have been made by the Council with many countries, including India, Yugoslavia and the Republic of China.

TRANSPORT

Private transport in Jordan consists of approximately 25,000 cars, trucks and motorcycles used by civilians. Above 85 per cent of inland freight is carried by road, 2 per cent by rail and 12 per cent by pipeline.

Jordan has a main, secondary and rural road network about 4,400 miles (7,050 km.) long—80 per cent of it good hard-surfaced roads. This system, maintained by the Ministry of Public Works, links major cities and towns as well as nearby countries. Local authorities are responsible for road repair. Syria is linked to Jordan via the Amman to Jerash-ar-Ramtha Highway. The Gulf of Aqaba is easily reached from Amman by the Ma'an Highway, a fairly new road and the principal route to the sea. From the town of Ma'an, the desert highway links Jordan with Saudi Arabia. The Amman-Jerusalem road passing through Na-ur is a major tourist artery. The government-owned Hejaz Railway, has completed a line connecting Hejaz with Aqaba, thus increasing revenues in the transport sector.

Into Jordan come major airlines from all parts of the world. The national airline,

Modern freighters from all over the world now berth at Aqaba, bringing much needed supplies to Jordan.

however, is run by Alia, otherwise known as the Royal Jordanian Airline, named after Hussein's eldest daughter. Alia's routes span almost all the Arab lands, and include London, African and European stops several times weekly.

Early in the 1960's, air transport became very active and the main airport in Amman and a small one in Jerusalem (built by Jordanians, now in Israeli hands) received all international carriers.

Jordan's Mediterranean sea trade before 1948 passed through Haifa. The Arab-Israeli clash of that era broke the link and Jordan's outlet became Beirut in friendly Lebanon. Expanding economy enabled the Jordanians to develop Aqaba.

The Ministry of Transport spends an average of 4,000,000 dinars a year on new road construction and maintenance on arterial highways. Travellers from afar have been heard to remark that Jordan has fine roads.

COMMUNICATIONS

The Hashemite Broadcasting Service, established in 1964, is financially independent, though it is responsible to the Minister of Culture and Information. Broadcasts in Arabic play 20 hours a day and those in English are transmitted 4 hours each day.

Jordan did not begin its television services until 1968, though the plans had been brewing from 1964 when suggestions were made to the government at that time.

In 1972, Jordan opened its first satellite station which brings live news to Jordan's television.

Jordanian television is received in Israel, Syria, southern Lebanon and parts of Saudi

Until completion of the new port facilities at Aqaba, merchandise was unloaded from freighters onto lighters (small, flat boats) to be carried ashore.

61

Aqaba has been built up considerably from the way it looked 20 years ago. This scene in 1954 was taken from an aircraft whose wing is visible at the left.

Arabia. Channel 6 is specially directed to the West Bank and Channel 3 to the rest of the country. Over 2,500,000 Jordanians dwell on 10 per cent of the land in the six urban areas, where the concentration is perfect for television. At least 80 per cent of the population sees the broadcasts, which start in the late afternoon, while 75 per cent of the people own television sets. Since a lot of the womenfolk are still bound by ancient traditions and do not step out alone, this indoor entertainment has brightened their life.

The press is free in Jordan. Four daily newspapers are issued, the most prominent ones being the Ad-Dustur and Al-Urdun in Arabic. Seven weekly newspapers and a daily are issued by the Arab National Union. Another weekly is published by the Armed Forces.

Numerous magazines, both monthly and quarterly, are published by government and non-governmental agencies. Some of the daily and weekly publications are issued under pri-

vate control. A magazine in English called "Jordan" comes out every 3 months under the direction of the Ministry of Tourism.

TOURISM

Tourism is a great advantage to Jordan's economy. The loss of the West Bank—Jerusalem, Bethlehem, Nablus, Jericho and all the other historical and religious places—was a severe blow to Jordanian tourism. Jordan is now devoting all its efforts to restore tourism to what it once was.

The rapid growth of tourism during the late 1950's and early 1960's was astounding. All the hotels were full and new hotels of international repute were in the process of being built. Later these too enjoyed a prosperous time. Foreign visitors increased from 132,000 to 617,000 and the visitors brought strength to the economy, besides the foreign exchange so desperately needed. Money poured in, raising that sector's funds to 11,300,000 Jordanian dinars. After the

These tourists on camels, with their guides, have spent 3 days and nights following caravan trails first established by the Roman legions 1,900 years ago. They are heading for camp at Wadi Rumm, where a hot meal, a shower and a good bed await them.

1967 war, tourism fell off and in 1971 a mere trickle of tourists came to Jordan, cutting the revenues way down.

For many years now there are tourist police in all the principal spots where tourists go. They speak fluent English and several other European languages and are not only helpful, but extremely gracious in their manner to strangers. Each year when the Tourist Festival season starts, these police are doubled, so that a visitor does not lose his way easily.

The festivals are advertised extensively with huge inviting posters, depicting scenes from the Camel & Horse Festival in April, the Water Ski Festival (April), the Olive and Orange Festival (November), the Jordanian Theatre Festival (May and November), and the Roman Amphitheatre performances each summer, with both local and foreign groups performing.

Tourists pass by the old walls of Amman.

INDEX